MOOGLI AND ME :)

MOOGLI AND ME :) OUR MAGICAL ADVENTURES

BY

LINDA MARIE GILLIAM

Hello there!

Do you like riddles?

Well I do, and so here is a riddle for you to solve: "What is enormous has 4 legs, eats hay, and grass... wears a saddle and bridle, and can trot?"

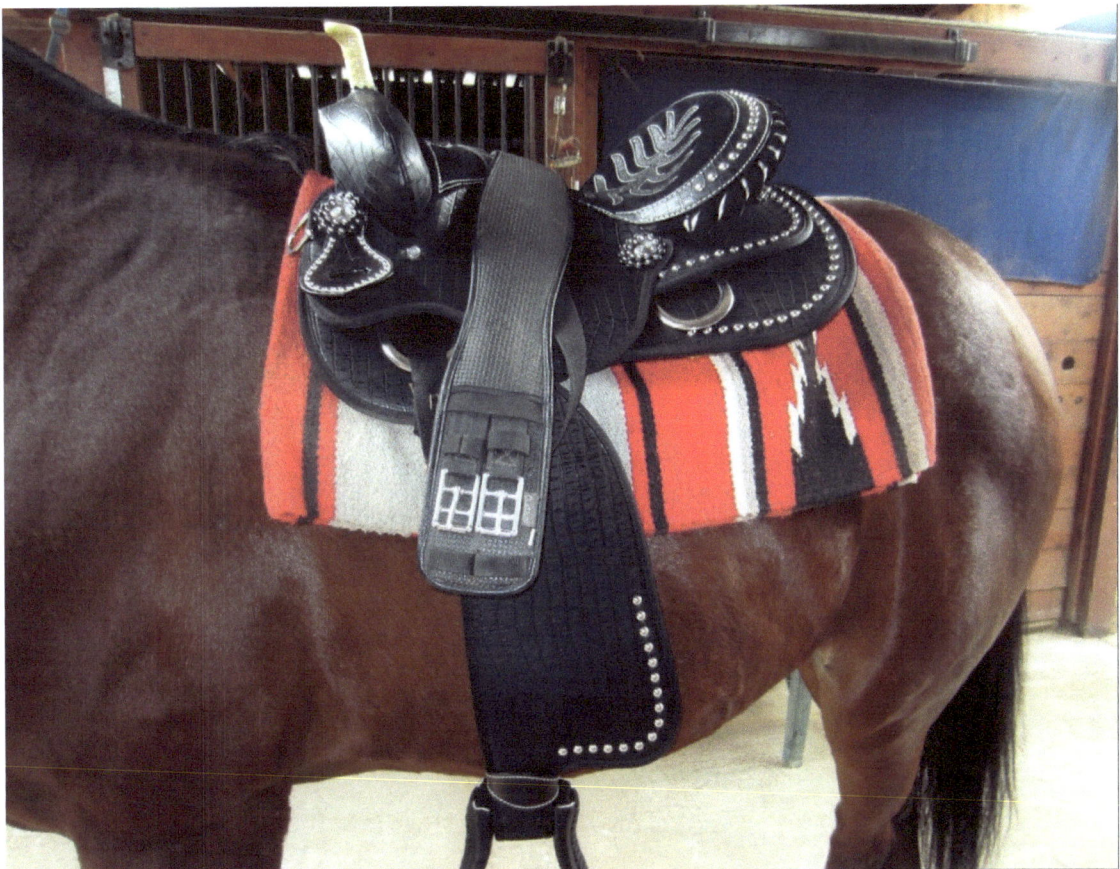

Do you give up?
Did you guess a horse?

If you did, you are correct and a very good listener to the clues. Good listening is so important to learning new things!

So...yes, it is ME, I am a *horse* and my name is "Pharaoh". I just turned 18 years old in January.

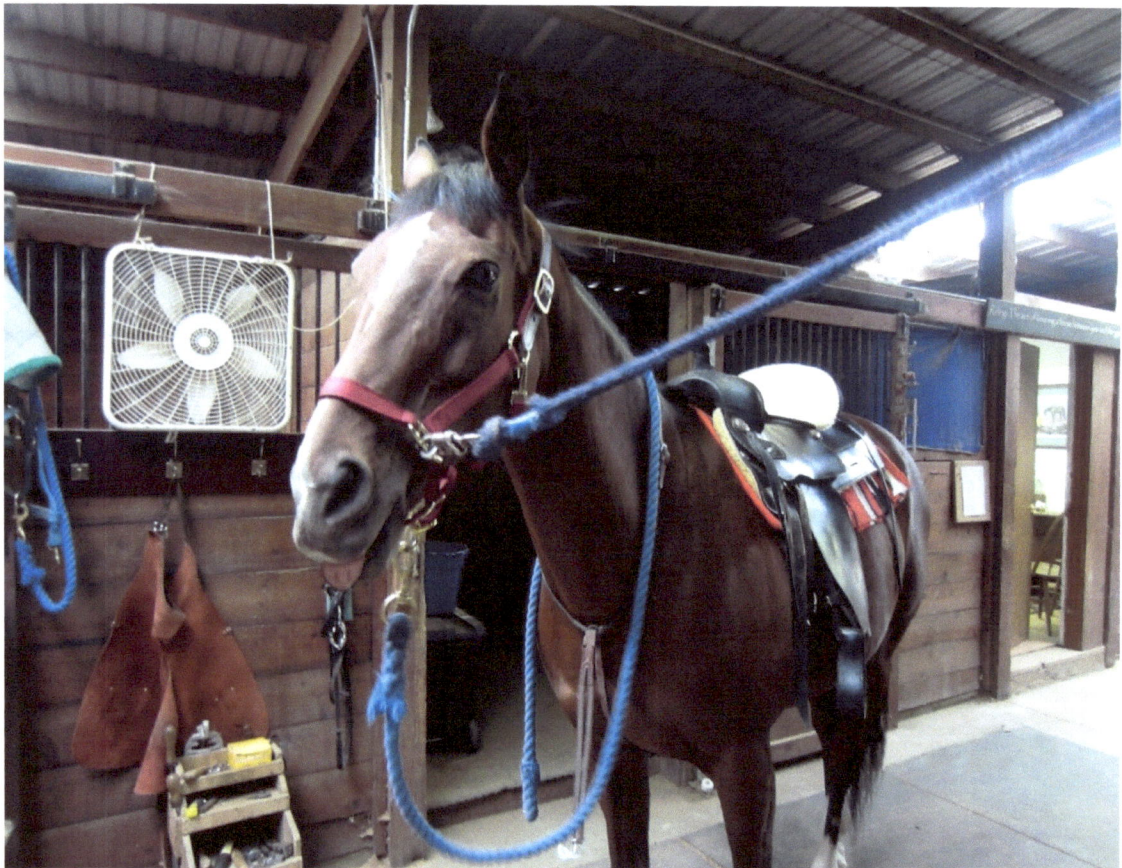

For a horse that is pretty old, although some horses can live to be almost 30.

Whew, that means if I can stay healthy, eat good foods, exercise, and take good care of myself, I will have many more years to kick up my heels and enjoy my friends. Speaking of good food...

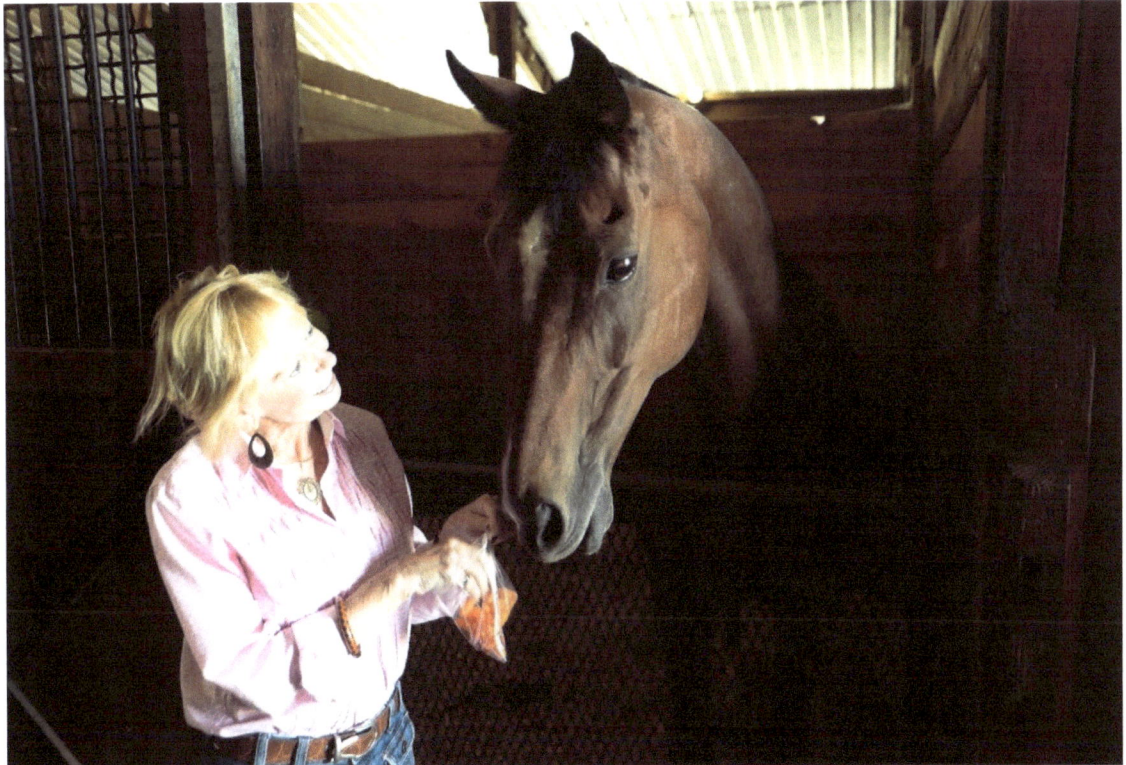

I know *carrots* are good for me!

By the way, I have a *mane* and tail with very big teeth, too. Did you already know that my mane is the hair around my head? Lions have manes, as well.

In order for me to stay healthy, each year our kind horse doctor, called a *veterinarian* comes to our barn to give us our shots or vaccinations. We know her as the "vet".

'

None of us like shots, but we know they are better than getting really sick from a disease, don't you agree? By the way, have you ever had to take your *pet to the vet?*

Hey…*that rhymes*, just like cat and hat, rat, and sat. Can you think of other words that rhyme? I think they are fun to say, don't you?

Let's get back to the vet; I often get off track when I am talking, oooops! I'm a HORSE after all.

Our vet gives every horse a "physical" or check-up, and cleans our teeth at the same time. Gosh, if she gives shots and cleans teeth, the vet is both a doctor and a dentist. What an important job!

My teeth always look dirty and _yellow_, but it is because of what I eat.

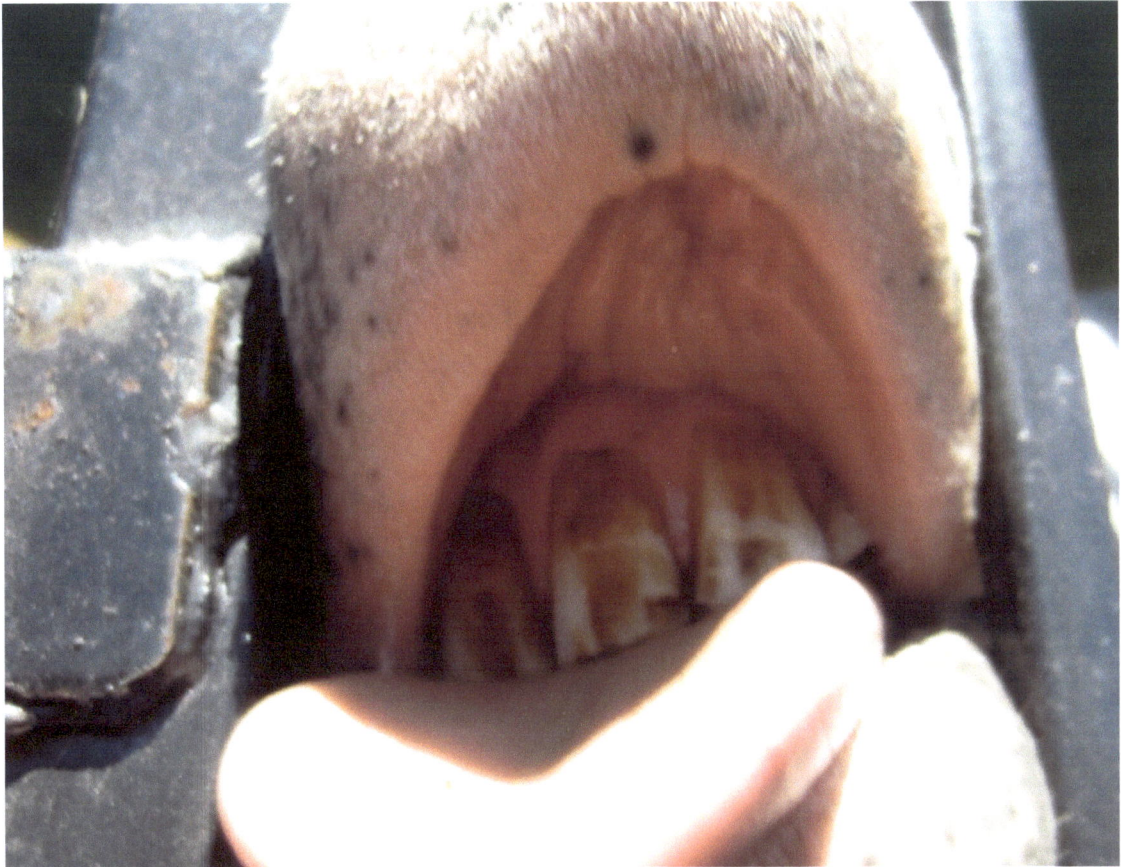

Since I heard that you already know some of your colors and color words, I will <u>underline</u> those words in our "Magical Adventure!"

Just so you know, color words help us to *describe* how things look. At the barn we sing that song you might already know?

"<u>Red</u> and <u>orange</u>, <u>green</u> and <u>blue</u>, shining

<u>yellow</u>, <u>purple</u>, too..

All the colors that I know…live up in the rainbow!

Except <u>brown</u> and <u>black</u>, <u>white</u> and <u>pink</u>…and are there more that you can think?"

I guess horses do get distracted, since I know I was talking about taking care of teeth. Moogli often says to me, "Pharaoh…Hocus Pocus you *can* focus!"

So, do you brush yours every day?

Some people even do something called "flossing", but I do not think that slippery stringy stuff would work for me without any hands! When you get older I hope you will floss to help your gums and teeth stay free of disease or cavities. To floss does not take that long to do, and food can easily get stuck in-between your teeth.

This left over food causes "*bacteria*", like germs... yuck! Unfortunately, I do not get to brush mine like I should. Here I am eating my healthy grain mush which obviously can get pretty messy.

If you had to eat with your mouth only, you might also look like this funny guy, which is me!

Luckily when I drink water, much of the sticky mush washes off.

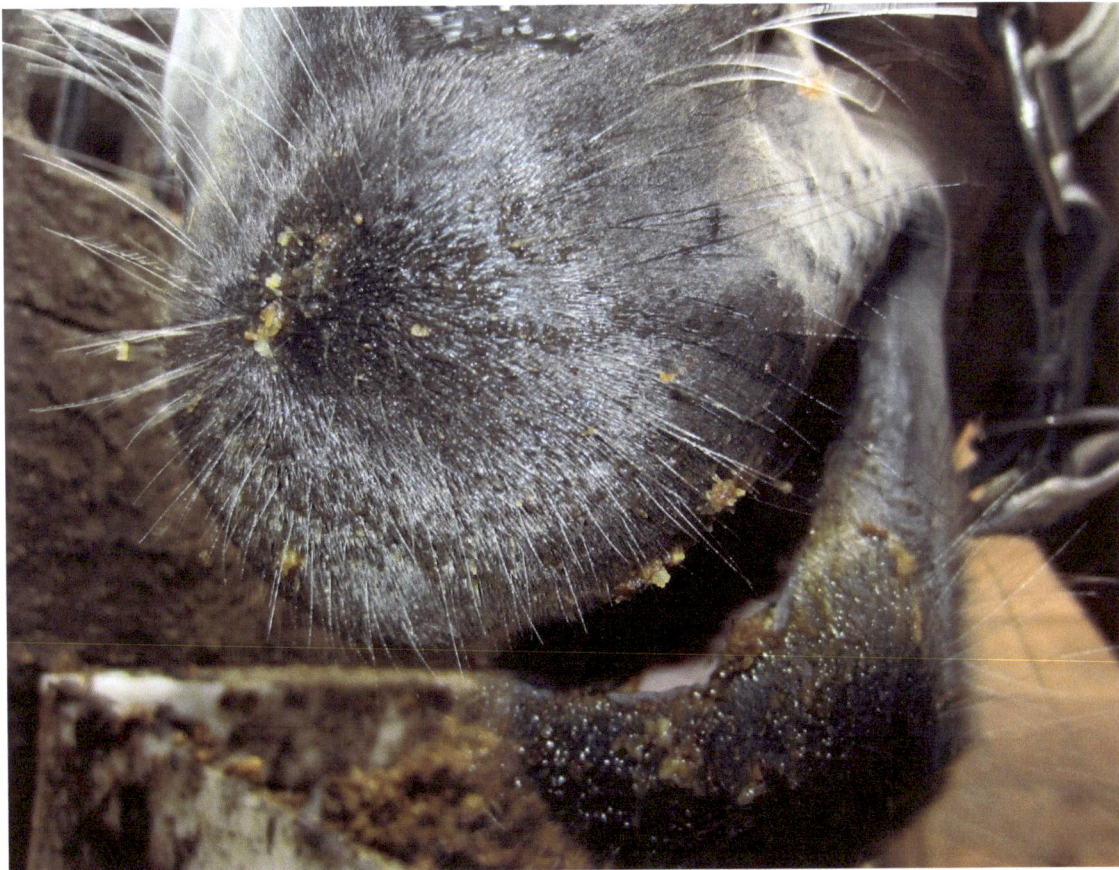

I bet you are glad you can brush your teeth every day, so you don't have to get any cavities, or fillings, right?

None of us like having their teeth drilled on if at all possible!

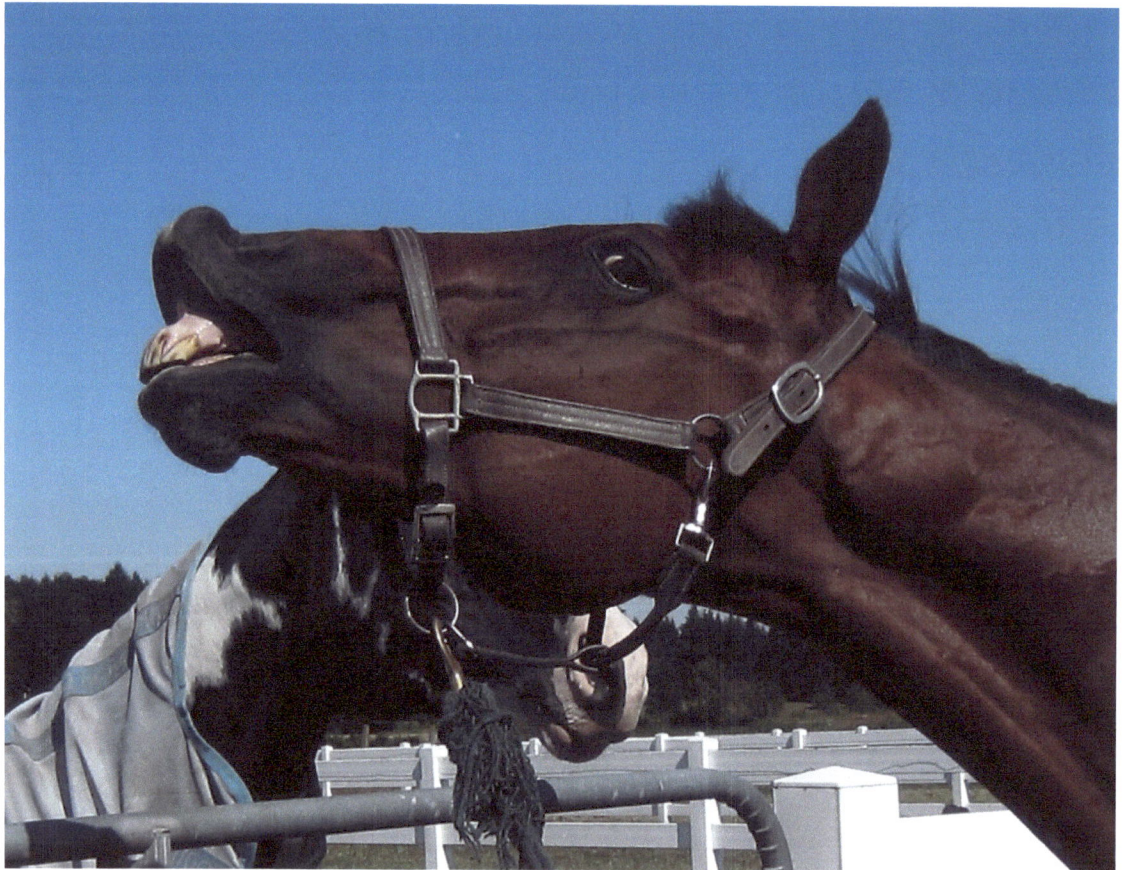

My teeth are always very <u>yellow</u>...SEEEEEEE?

When the light shines just right on them, they are the color of <u>yellow</u> butter. But sometimes with eating all that grain, you will see some <u>brown</u> on my teeth as well.

I like to show them off, but others say they are "Gross"!!! All horses have teeth sort of like mine, however.

At least my gums are <u>pink</u>, and that shows they are healthy!

Looking at my pictures tells me I certainly do need a shave of my long whiskers! You could call me "fuzzy face" by the way I look.

Since I cannot shave my own face, my humans do that for me. They use an electric razor, and the *buzz* of it sort of tickles my nose. The vibration makes such a funny noise and very strange feelings on my skin.

Maybe your dad, uncle, older brother or grandfather uses an electric razor to shave? Some men prefer to use the razor blade with shaving cream for a closer shave. "No thanks", I say!

On no, there I go again, getting off the topic of dental care, and brushing teeth.

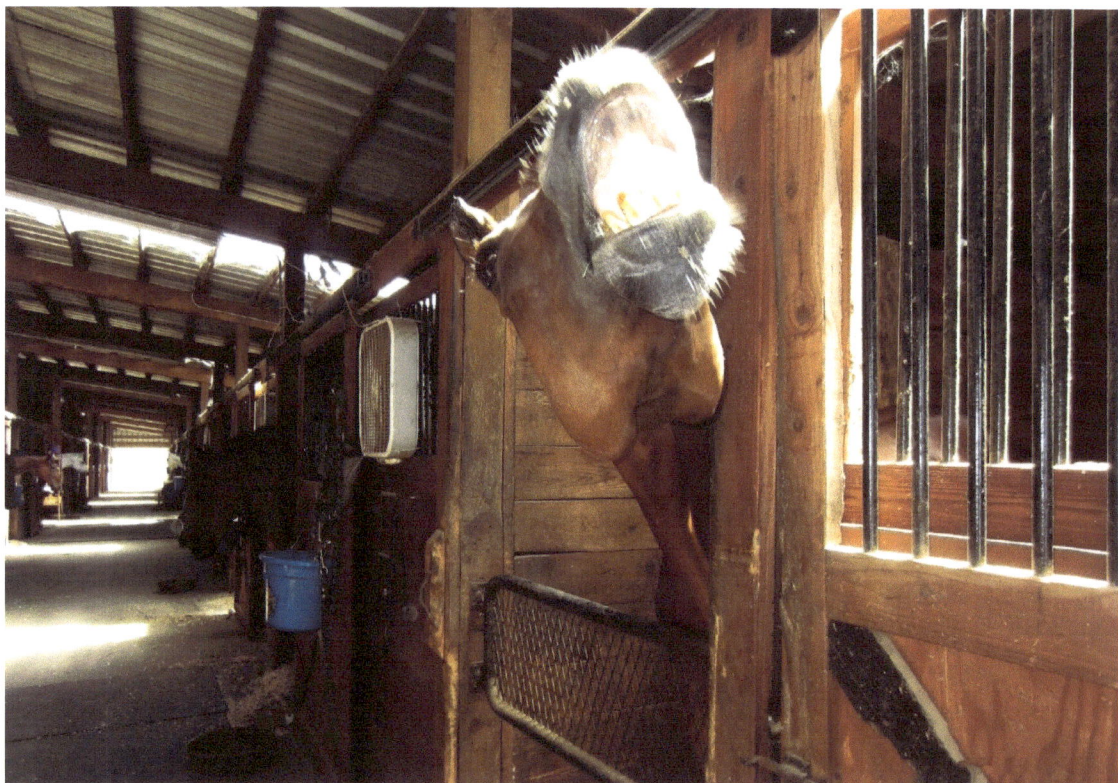

Silly me!

I won't even worry about being off *track*, when telling you things, because for so many years I was on *track*, while I was a racehorse. Get it?

I just had to throw in that joke, too.

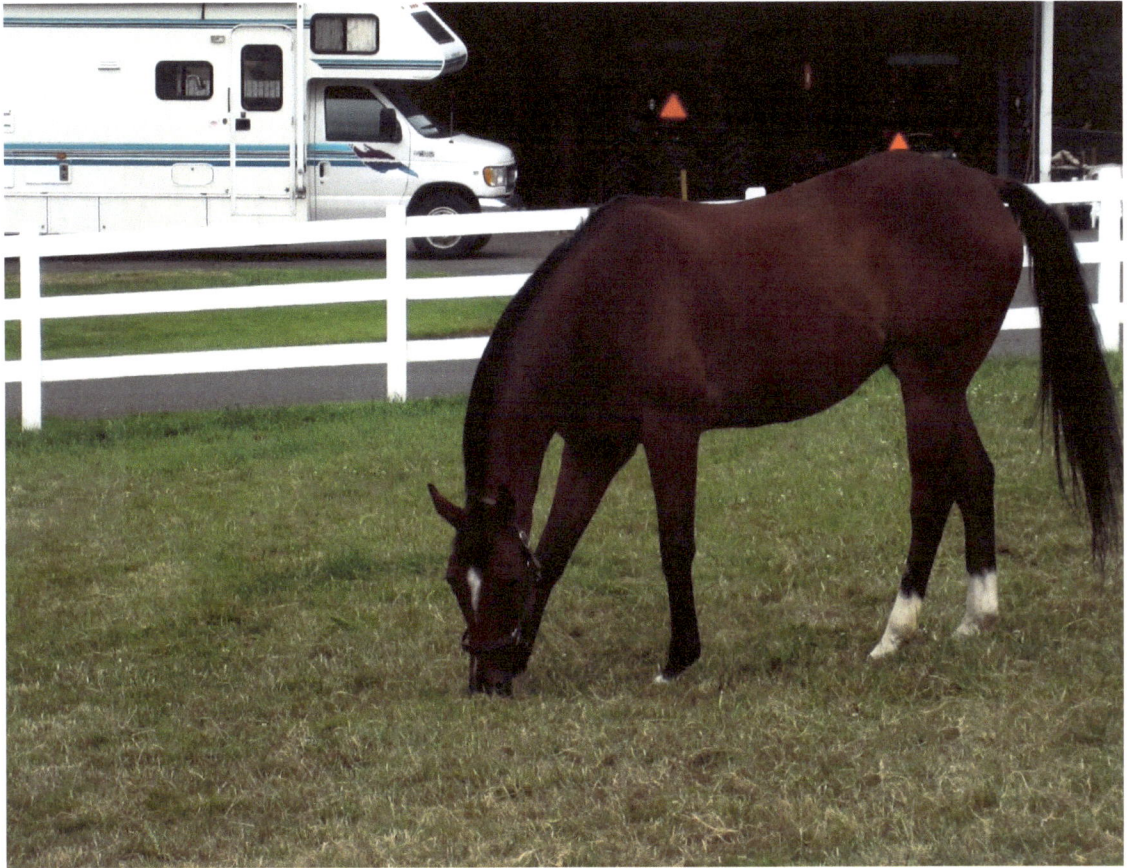

Sometimes my teeth get a little <u>green</u> as well, from the yummy grass I get to eat in the pasture outside.

In a way the grass is like eating my *vegetables*, I guess. Although my body also needs lots of grain, vitamins, and hay, I know when the grass is growing tall, that is my favorite thing to eat.

Many kids do <u>not</u> eat or even like their veggies, I heard... but I am here to tell you how good they are for your body.

So, what is your *favorite vegetable*?

Is it string beans, broccoli, spinach, peas or bananas?

Ha! I am hoping you know that a banana is a fruit, <u>not</u> a vegetable! Can you name some other fruits?

The humans all say that they need to eat their fruits and vegetables to stay healthy.

I know I *love* to eat carrots and apples...so that would be a vegetable with a fruit, right?

I do love grass, even when it is not very <u>green</u>.

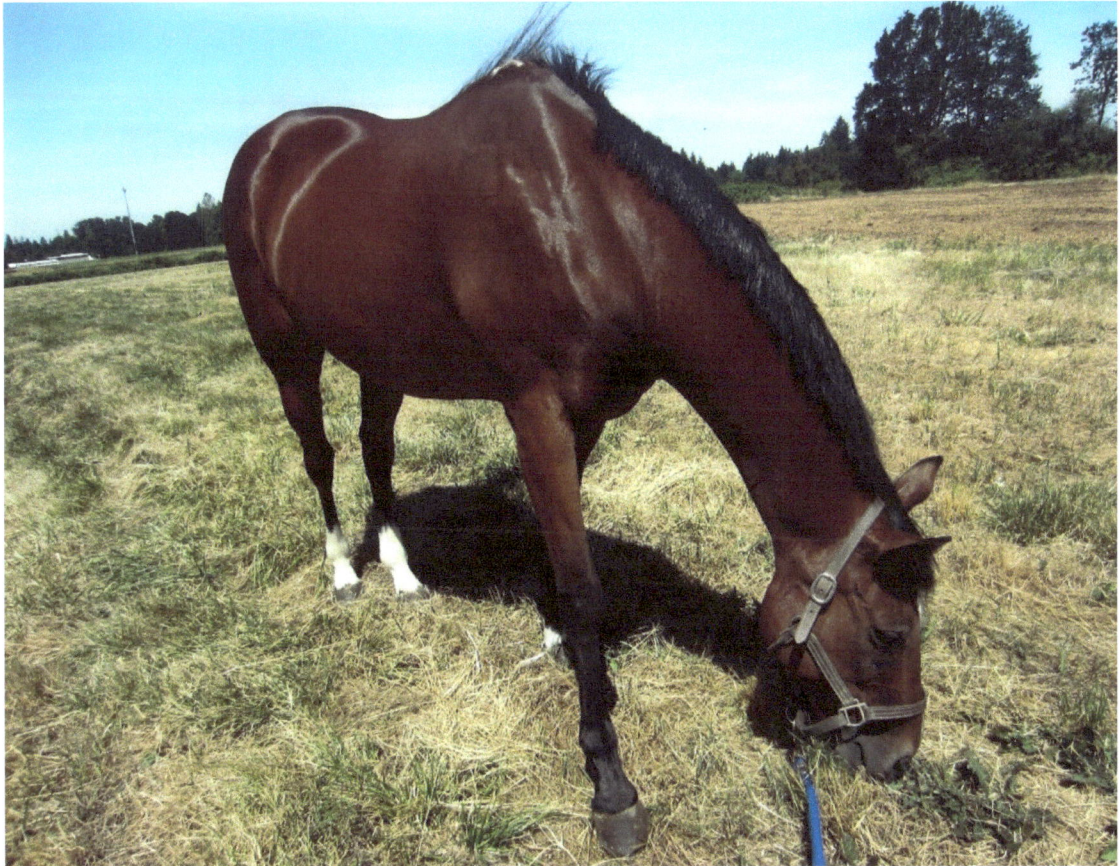

When the weather stays hot or dry, with no rain, we have to eat dried out grass. Sometimes you get what you get, and don't throw a fit!

Okay, let's see if you can get the _next_ riddle I have for you?

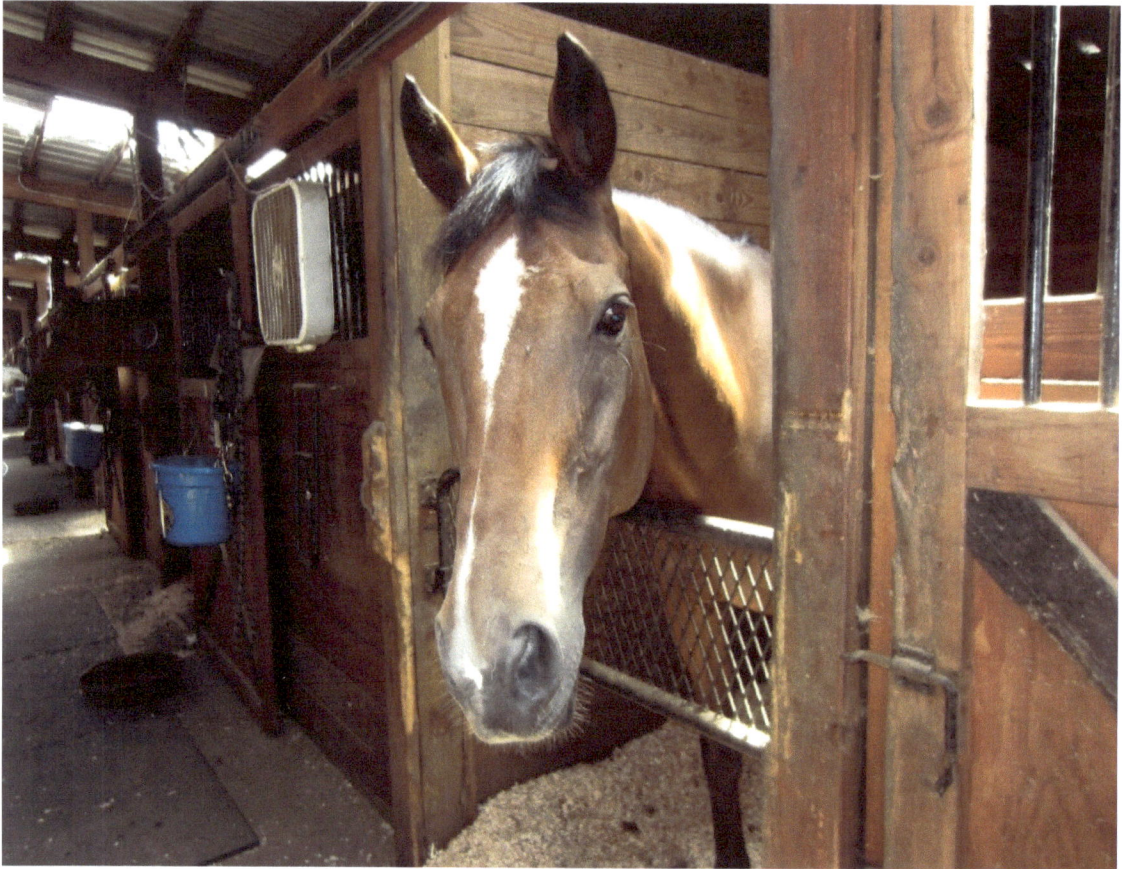

"What has black and white fur, 4 legs, eats fish, and lives in our barn to chase away the mice?"

Did you guess a cat named "Moogli"? (That riddle was easier I think.)

Oh wait, I have not introduced you to Magical Moogli, have I?

Well he is more than just a cat. Moogli is my *very best* friend! In reality, he is quite a handsome cat as you can see in this photo!

So this beautiful cat is Moogli, and not only my *best friend*, but always around the stables trying to help others. He cheers up everyone, at the same time.

Moogli has very soft <u>black</u> and <u>white</u> fur, gentle <u>green-yellow</u> eyes, and a little <u>pink</u> nose. His whiskers are long and <u>white</u>, but he never shaves like me!

OK, no more riddles for now, since I want to tell you a story about "Moogli and Me: Our Magical Adventures."

First of all, who would think that a huge horse and a tiny cat could be best of friends? You might think that a cat would get under my feet or hooves, and get squished like a pancake?

Yikes!

If that happened, I would feel terrible, but I bet Moogli would feel worse as a *"kitty pancake"*! That is not even funny to joke about, is it?

A cat might be too small for me to ever notice or care about, since I am a very gigantic horse!

Well, Moogli is so smart he stays away from my hooves, and knows where he needs to sit or stand to talk to me.

He is often up on a <u>brown</u> table "doing his laundry", as he calls it...which is cleaning his fur.

With our barn so dusty and dirty, Moogli is constantly licking his fur to make it shiny again.

I often wonder how his little *pink* tongue does not get tired of doing this over and over; since the dirt is everywhere he goes.

Sometimes the sawdust that is put in our stalls gets on his fur too, and then he has to spit that out with the dust!

Ick!

Many times Moogli sweeps up around the barn to help keep our stables looking nice and neat. Others help him since it is such a huge job!

I would bet you get to help at home or in the classroom, too?

I hear that humans *really appreciate helpers*. Even if you are little or young, there is always something you can do to help out, right?

Now Moogli and I want to talk about how important friends are for all of us.

Maybe you have a *best friend* that you love to talk to and play with? That good friend might be someone in your church, neighborhood or even at your school?

Friends *share* their books, bikes, toys, video games, food, and anything else that might make their special friend feel happy.

They should do the *same* for you, if they are truly a best friend, right?

Sometimes you first need to talk about how to take *good care* of anything that you share together, and how to take care of it as if it was your *very own*.

Friends are very important to have, that's for sure! They can make your life so much more enjoyable, and worthwhile.

These human friends are Amy and C.J. They both have horse friends living here too.

 A good friend can share your stories, dreams, and adventures.

They can *understand* how you are feeling, and know what to do to make you feel better.

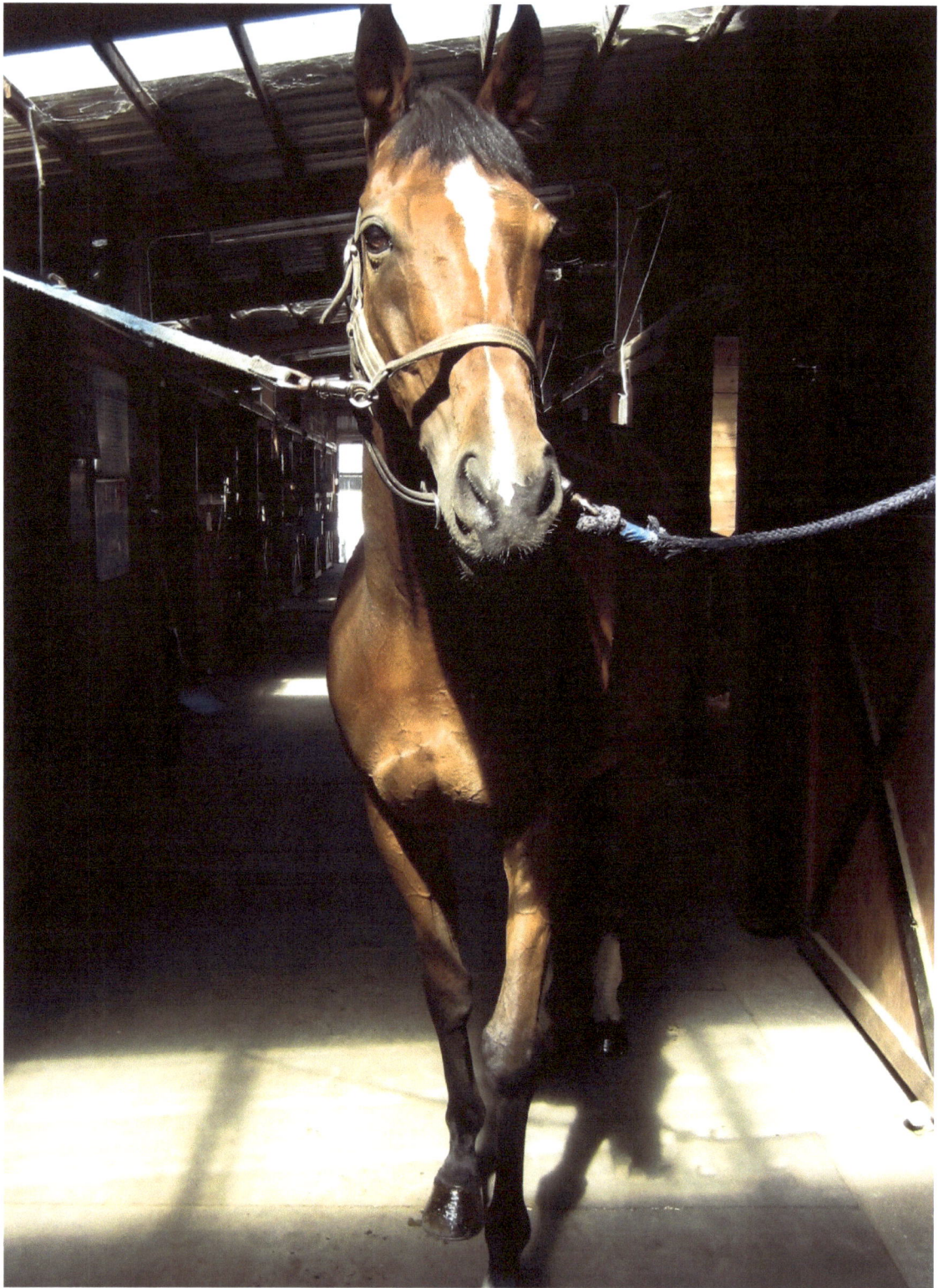

Just so you know, I am a former racehorse and *famous* for being the Great, Great Grandson of

"Seattle Slew" and "Secretariat". (Both are very well-known race horses that won many races). My name when I raced was "Kid Chrome". I won many races myself.

You might think I would only have other race horses for my friends, since my relatives were like "Rock Stars" when it came to horse racing?

Well, this is just *not* true, even though I did something really important, I am never stuck up or a bragger. Besides, I know that behaving that way would be rude, and *not* help me to make the friends I want.

Moogli and I think it is easy to make friends, although sometimes it is *harder* to keep them. You have to work at it.

By the way, just because others may look a little different than you do, it does *not* mean they cannot become your great friends!

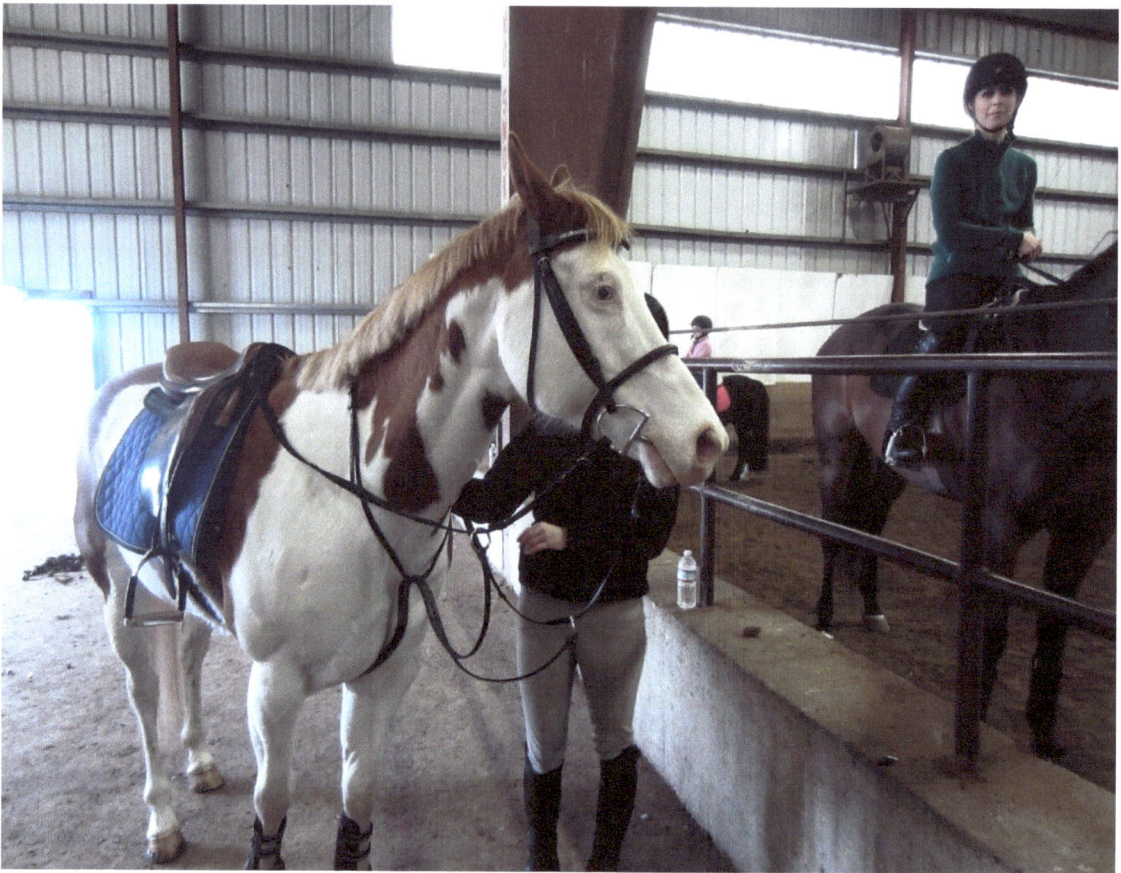

This brown and white "paint" horse *looks so different* than I do, yet we are still super friends.

But since we are both horses. I guess the friendship might be easier to understand, than my friendship with Moogli the cat?

Let's just say upfront, Moogli is an extremely handsome cat, and although we certainly do look

VERY different, eat different things, and speak different languages...we still can communicate with each other perfectly, (or "purrfectly" as Moogli would say).

Did you get my joke?

Moogli seems to understand me, and loves to visit and play every day, even when I am in my stall or tied up.

He always makes my day go better and makes me smile! I know we will stay friends forever...like humans say, we are "BFFs" = *Best Friends Forever!*

I think it is important that you get to know some very *special people* in my life.

Moogli's human is called "Verne", and Verne takes great care of *all of us* at the barn or stable.

Verne often lets us out of our stall to run and play, for *exercise*. You could call it our recess! He feeds us hay and grain every day! Verne also cleans the "poopy p-u" stalls, puts in fresh sawdust, and gives us new metal shoes to protect our hooves or feet.

We all love Verne!

(People who shoe horses are "ferriers".)

Moogli is supervising Verne, to make sure this horse stands very, very still.

First the hoof is clipped, like your toenail must be cut off if it grows too long.

Next, the *metal horseshoes* have to be formed to the horses' hoof and then nailed into the hoof carefully.

Luckily our hoof is like your toenails with no feeling…or nerves, to hurt us when they get cut.

You might say hair is the same as toenails? Neither of them hurt when cut off. That is a very good thing this horse thinks!

With all the *responsibilities* Verne has, he still loves teaching the other young and old humans how to ride the horses correctly.

Verne is an *excellent* rider, and has won many, many awards in Canada.

Can you find *Canada* on a map? Is it close to the United States?

"Ashley" is a younger human with two different horses at the barn.

She rides and jumps very well. Ashley has lessons often with Verne so she can *improve* her skills.

By the way, riding is *not* just sitting on our backs saying, "giddy-up-horsie!"

This is my human, "Linda", and although she is older, she still *loves* to ride and play with me.

You might notice the saddles look a little different? Well, Ashley has an *"English Saddle"*, while Linda rides with a *"Western Saddle"*.

Linda told me she wants to have the saddle with a *horn*... not for "honking", but for holding onto if she loses her balance.

Did you like my funny joke?

Some humans do silly things like jumping over sticks or poles with us! Who thought that up, I wonder?

This horse is trying to roll the stick over. He knows, with this stick pole being so low, he says, "It would be easy-peasy to jump over the pole with all four hooves".

Hey, let's see if you know the type of saddle he is wearing? Look closely! How can you tell?

Did you look for the *horn*, and bigger *stirrups*? Oh, *stirrups* are what your feet rest on for better balance.

Jumping is a very exciting sport, but the riders need to make sure they wear helmets and *protective* riding gear.

Just like Moogli and I hope you do when riding your bike or skateboard? Do you always make sure to wear a *helmet* to protect your head? That is so very *important for safety*, as you already know?

Besides, we cannot *always know* what might happen next, even if we are good at some sport or skill.

This horse is jumping in a contest, and decides at the last minute he does <u>not</u> want to jump! That sudden stopping is called "refusing a jump", and can be very, *very dangerous* if the rider falls off.

Moogli says it looks like that horse is "putting on the brakes"!

Now we want to get back to more about Moogli. Luckily for Moogli, he can come and go as he pleases.

He has the run of the barn and can go from place to place without a human and a rope.

That would be fun, I think.

But, unfortunately I cannot.

Moogli told me he is only 5 years old, and his job is to get rid of all the mice that hide in the hay.

The *"stinky mice"* also make a mess of the hay that we horses are supposed to eat. Those *naughty mice* even fill their fat tummies with the grain that is meant for the horses. How dare them!!!

No wonder I love Moogli! If I did not get my yummy grain each day, I might not stay as healthy as I am, with such a shiny <u>brown</u> coat as in this picture with the pretty <u>blue</u> sky, <u>green</u> trees and <u>white</u> fences. Moogli and I love to be outside!

In reality, I suppose Moogli is my best friend because he always comes by my stall to visit and see how I am doing each day. Good friends look out for one another, right?

Even on party days, Moogli shares pizza with all of us. It makes us sad, but some of the cats seem to fight with each other, yet Moogli tries to get along with everyone.

I really do admire him, since none of us like bullies.

Do you like children who pick on you, tease you, or take away your toys? I did not think so! I do believe that if everyone would share, take turns, and consider the *other person's feelings*...life would be so much nicer for all of us.

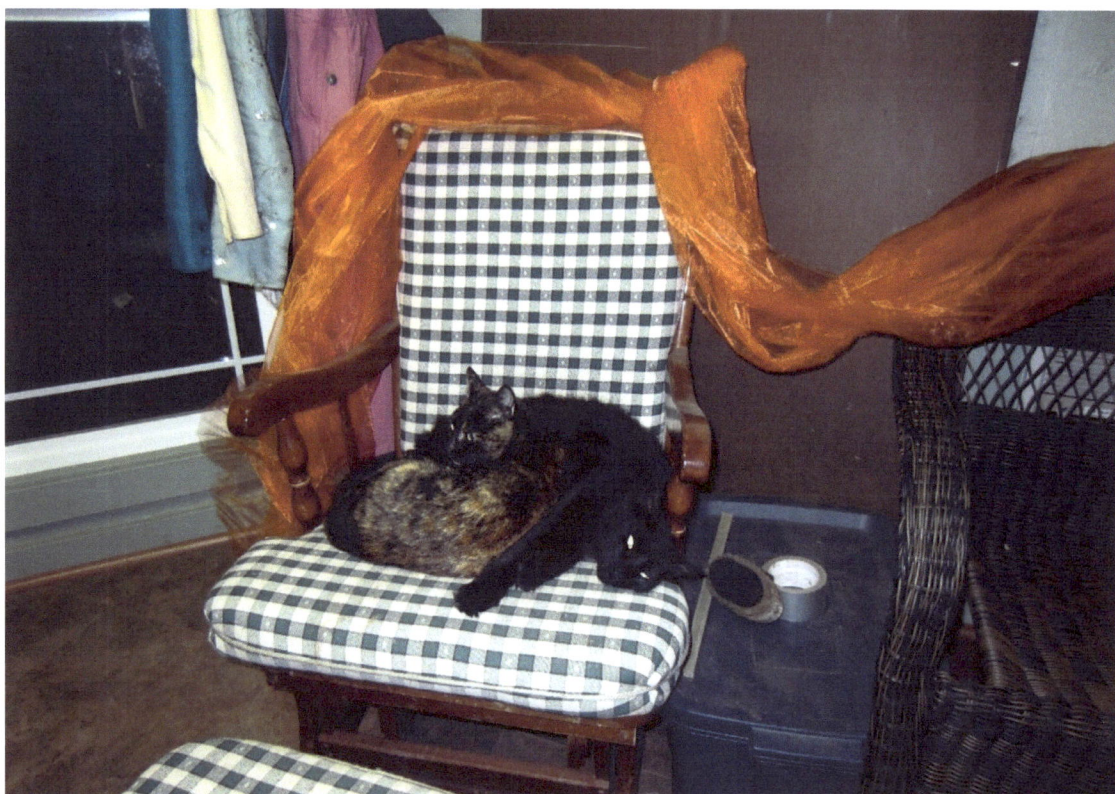

We even have some horses here at our barn that tries to be the BOSS of all of us. Those horses do not have many, if any, friends I notice.

There is a horse at our barn named *"Brutus"* that is always like that. He bites, kicks, and puts his ears back most of the time, as if he is having a very bad day. He has to stay in a fenced area by himself most of the time.

Moogli and I often wonder why he is so grumpy, and why Brutus does not try harder to get along.

Maybe he ate something that does not agree with him?

Or could it be he was never shown *how* to be nice or how to make friends?

One day, my human, Linda, talked us into trying to find out *why* Brutus was being so bad and mean to everyone.

She told us maybe Brutus did not have a happy home before we met him, that he does not feel well, or is a bully because no one likes him!

We never thought of that, so decided to be nicer to Brutus and see if he *changed his behavior*.

What did we have to lose?

My other nice human, *"Robin"*, agreed with Linda.

Therefore, Moogli and I decided we would both talk to Brutus and smile each day when we saw him.

We asked Brutus to play with us, gave him a carrot and found out Linda was right! Brutus did <u>not</u> have a very nice life when he was younger.

Brutus told us that he had lost his daddy when he was very small and became so *angry.*

The angrier he got, the fewer friends he had, and so he decided he did not need *anyone!*

He thought by being a bully he could feel *more powerful,* and not show us how hurt he really was.

Unfortunately, this bad behavior made his life *more miserable*, and each day was as bad as the last…or even worse. Brutus was ready to give up ever having any friends! All the other horses ignored him.

You will *never* guess what happened after we talked to Brutus? He does not seem like the same horse. Now Brutus is so much happier; he does not bite, kick or put his ears back, unless the wind is blowing and a storm is coming.

He looks better, feels better, and has many friends... just because we took the time to see why he was acting the way he was.

My human, Linda, told Moogli and Me how we were showing COMPASSION and EMPATHY to Bully Brutus.

Wow, what do those big words *mean* anyway?

Compassion and empathy were shown by us trying to understand Brutus and his reasons for behaving badly.

And she also mentioned that even if Brutus *never changed* (but hopefully he would for the better), we could at least know we did our very best to help him... right?

Maybe you could help someone at your church, school, or in the neighborhood, that does not have many friends?

They might enjoy their life more, by you doing what we did for "Brutus the Bad Bully", who is now happier to be called: *"Brutus, Our Best Buddy"!*

Pharaoh, Moogli and Linda all love knowing they helped Brutus change, and all 3 of them hope *there is someone* you will help as well?

By using your better understanding now of Compassion and Empathy, you can help everyone you know live a happier and less frustrating life everywhere.

We all want the fighting and violence in our world to end! This fighting makes Pharaoh, Moogli and Linda *very* sad!

Their wish is for you to use your new words of compassion and empathy daily. Then, hopefully, the world will learn to have more love for all of us!

Remember: Kindness is the key to happiness!

Being kind to others really makes you feel good inside, and also those you have been kind to feel *even* better.

Moogli and Linda love it when I do my "silly giggles" to make Brutus smile again! Our whole stable seems like such a happier place to be now... for all of us.

So, maybe you can talk about what you learned in this story told by Pharaoh, Moogli, and all their friends?

This is "Buckaroo Barbie" showing off the book you just read, *with more coming soon*:

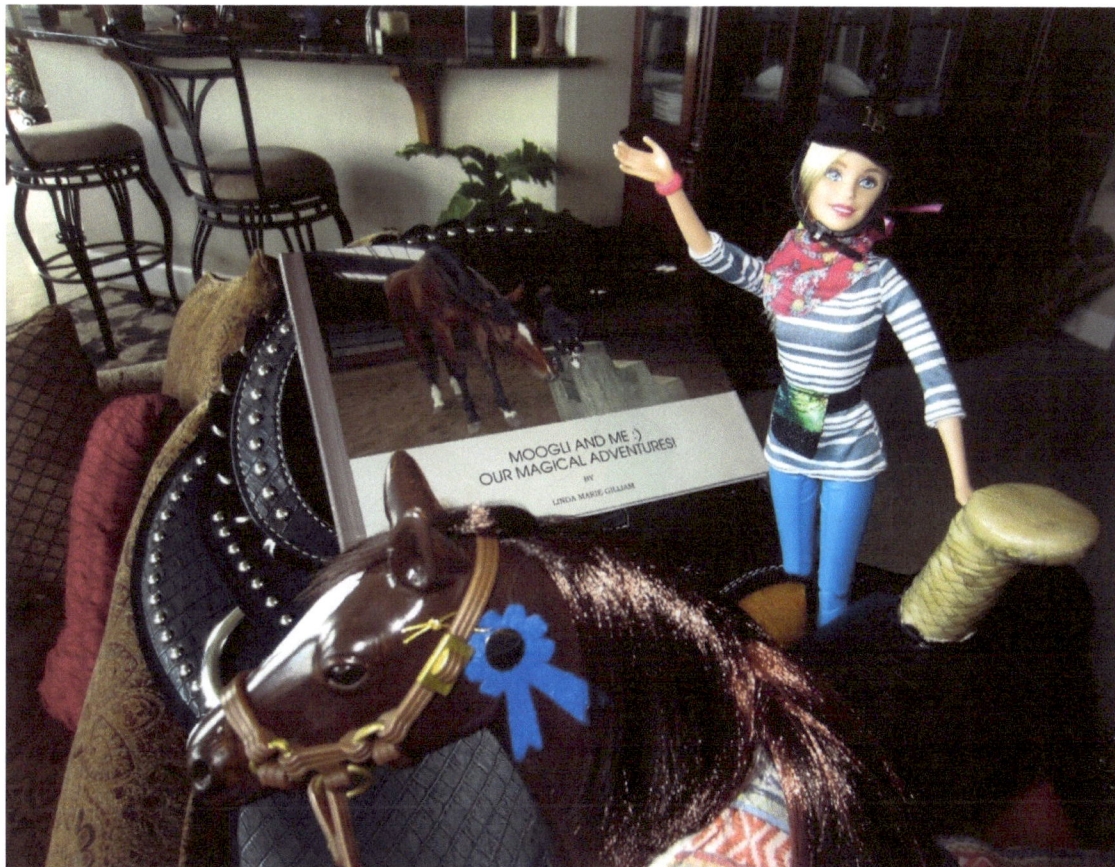

Moogli and Me: Our Magical Adventures!

By   LINDA MARIE GILLIAM ☺

follow us on YouTube.Com channel Moogli and Me!

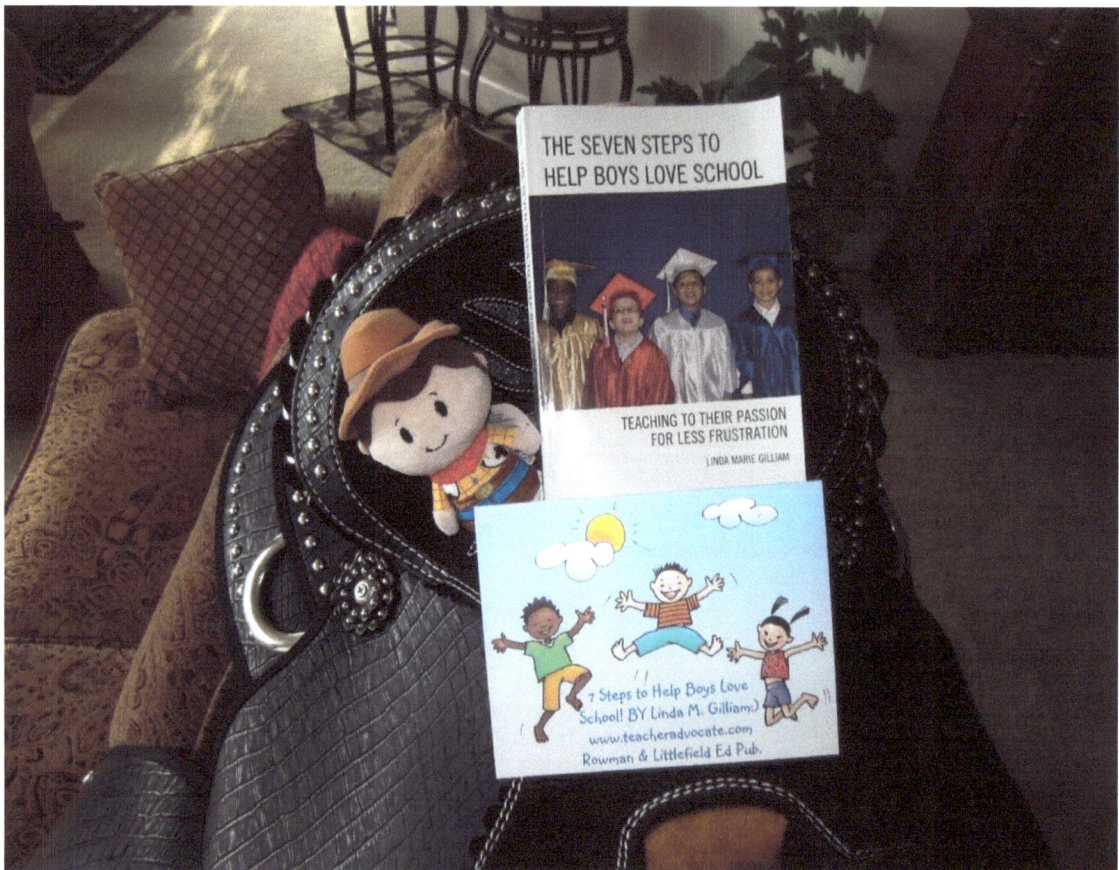

This "Happy Boy" is showing you the very first book that Linda wrote... which is for parents, and teachers/ the book helps children to *love* learning and is entitled:

THE SEVEN STEPS TO HELP BOYS LOVE SCHOOL: TEACHING TO THEIR PASSION FOR LESS FRUSTRATION!

PUBLISHED BY ROWMAN & LITTLEFIELD EDUCATIONAL DEPARTMENT 2015

www.ingramcontent.com/pod-product-compliance
Lightning Source LLC
Chambersburg PA
CBHW041545040426
42447CB00002B/44